IVAR THE B(

Myths Legends

KIV Books

Copyright © 2018

Disclaimer

This book is designed to provide condensed information. It is not intended to reprint all the information that is otherwise available, but instead to complement, amplify and supplement other texts. You are urged to read all the available material, learn as much as possible and tailor the information to your individual needs.

Every effort has been made to make this book as complete and as accurate as possible. However, there may be mistakes, both typographical and in content. Therefore, this text should be used only as a general guide and not as the ultimate source of information. The purpose of this book is to educate.

The author or the publisher shall have neither liability nor responsibility to any person or entity regarding any loss or damage caused, or alleged to have been caused, directly or indirectly, by the information contained in this book.

Table of Contents

Introduction

In the following pages we will explore the life and exploits of one of the most fearsome Vikings who has ever walked the earth. We should note that Ivar the Boneless is a complex individual. The records that talk about him are quite conflicting as they often are with mythical and historical figures.

This book will take a close look to his origins, family and notable exploits. We will also catch a glimpse into the possibilities of his demeanor and behavior without moving away from the fact that he is one of the most ruthless men to ever invade England in the 9th century. We will also point out areas where the records conflict one another and thus show how difficult it is for historians to reconstruct the life of even a prominent Viking due to the lack of definitive records.

It is our hope that you'll enjoy this book and learn many new things about Ivar the Boneless!

Who is Ivar the Boneless?

"My whole story is straight mythical. It's tangible, but it's also what life could be."

– Travis Scott

If you have been dabbling in the world of the Vikings or maybe you may have watched Viking movies or have been following the History Channel's TV series, Vikings, then you most likely have come across one of the most curious of these seafaring folk – Ivar nicknamed "The Boneless."

His existence cannot be denied due to the many different sources that allude to him. However, just like other historical figures, even though his existence is truthfully indisputable, exact details about the man, his personality, and character, is limited. He is truly a shadowy and illusive figure.

A huge portion about the things we know about Ivar the Boneless comes from the sagas from Scandinavia. Well, more particularly from the saga about his father, who is also another famous Viking by the name of Ragnar Lothbrok – the Viking who sacked Paris. In fact, the entire family does carry quite a reputation for themselves.

A Legendary Family and Bloodline

Ragnar Lothbrok (or Lodbrok) himself was an ambitious and worthy seafarer. He was notorious as he was great. The saga of Ragnar Lothbrok actually serves as a sequel to the saga of Volsunga – one of the Icelandic sagas. Ragnar's saga tells of his exploits, his love pursuits – which includes his marriages to Thora and also Aslaug (Ivar's mother), the birth of his sons (which includes Ivar's birth) and also their various adventures.

You can say that the entire Lothbrok household is truly extraordinary. Even Ivar's brothers themselves had their reputations precede them wherever they went. In fact, their infamy even won them battles even before the fighting had begun. This was the case when the Danes led by Ivar were outnumbered in one battle in southern England yet they won because of the reputation of their commander – we'll cover that battle later in this book.

The Curious Viking

One of the most fascinating things about Ivar the Boneless is the fact that he is full of contradictions. Well, to clarify, at least what the records and annals say about him was contradictory. One source would tell you one thing about him, which would make sense, and then a total information turn around would occur with another source telling you something totally opposite.

For instance, his epithet *The Boneless* is quite debated. Some take it quite literally, that he was a cripple born with a genetic bone disease. On the other hand another source would describe Ivar the Boneless as one of the largest Vikings ever seen. In fact some describe him as one of the berserkers who can conjure up a blood thirsty rage.

Some describe him as being 9 feet tall while others would describe him as 3 feet tall borne into battle on top of a shield on the shoulders of his men. Some sources describe Ivar as a raging warrior who can slay dozens at the head of his army while another source would describe him as a calm, sly, witty, and brilliant strategist who could outwit the enemy. Some would even describe him as a master of words who could persuade kings, which is hardly a trait of a berserking cold blooded killer.

Sometimes he would be described as an impotent – unable to produce offspring. On the other hand some would describe him as having his curious way with women – that is he was extra flexible in bed. It was also told that when news came about his father Ragnar's death at the hands of King Ælla that his brothers and the rest of his companions were enraged yet Ivar listened patiently all the while hatching a plan for revenge. Another contradiction is that he lived a life of violence and ironically he died in peace.

The Fearsome Warlord

His real name would have been Ivar Ragnarsson yet he was often called Ivar the Boneless or Ivar inn Beinlausi (Old Norse) or Ívarr hinn Beinlausi (also Old Norse). His name in Old English is rendered as Hyngwar, and you will find several records with his name spelled as such.

Together with his brothers he led the greatest army of Danes to England not just for revenge but to conquer. The only record of the acts of Ivar the Boneless come from the very monks, whose monasteries the Vikings raided, who survived and lived to tell the tale. They left behind short descriptions of the attack, of the men who ravaged and burned the land, and how swift and fearsome was the devastation that they incurred. Nevertheless, their records were sketchy and they only give us glimpses of this mythical Viking warlord.

The annals that we can draw from to learn about Ivar's war tactics and strategy come from English and Irish chronicles. However, they are enough to convey to us how rapid and how overwhelming the Viking invasion really was. Village after village fell – and they all fell quickly. The army would then be known as the Great Heathen Army amongst the Christians. And at the head of that army is Ivar – one of the most fearsome and dangerous men of the 9th century.

The years leading to 865 AD, the people of England have become used to Viking raids. To them these people were merely pirates who pillaged, robbed, and killed. So they paid them little mind even though the threat was truly serious. That was until Ivar landed with his army. They were not there to raid and get treasures – they came to conquer, they came to rule.

This army that Ivar brought with him was larger than any army they have seen in centuries. It was even larger than the army headed by William the Conqueror. Note that the annals come from different regions and different towns. These chroniclers don't even know each other; however they used the same words to describe the leader of this invading army.

They attributed qualities to him as *crudelisimus* which translates to "most cruel." They also described him as one who is *invictusimus* which means he was unconquerable. That means he has never lost a battle since his campaign. When you combine those two qualities – someone who is absolutely cruel and someone who has never lost a fight and who can't be conquered then you know that doom is at your doorstep.

Contemporary chronicles of Ivar the Boneless don't actually give us all the details. That means we don't really know who Ivar the man really is. The best thing that we can do is to put some pieces of the puzzle together of what we know from different fragmentary records and also the opinions and knowledge of scholars.

One of the biggest sources of course is the Viking sagas. But remember that these sagas were written at least 300 years after the chronicled events had occurred.

Origins of the Boneless

"Enlightened despots are mythical creatures; real despots seem more interested in stealing money or installing their sons after them."

−Elliott Abrams

Birth and Mother's Curse

The birth of Ivar the Boneless is a mix of both legend and folklore. We have already mentioned elsewhere that the primary sources that are available to us that describe him and his origins are the Scandinavian sagas. Of course Ivar's movements during the war can be contrasted and compared with contemporary records written by his enemies. However, tracing his origins and earlier history will be a bit more difficult since you have no other sources to compare them to.

Even the sagas offer a variety of detail. For instance, the Hattalykill, a poem that was probably written somewhere around the middle of the 12th century, describe Ivar to be someone as "without any bones at all" which of course is impossible. Of course sagas and other stories can get embellished as the years go by. Note that the Hattalykill was written several centuries later after Ivar's death.

The largest amount of detail we can gather about the man's birth is from his father's saga − Ragnar's saga. According to the sagas, his birth was as violent as his life. His mother, princess Aslaug, was the second wife (in other records she is the third wife) of the current king, Ragnar.

The place of his birth is unknown but it is estimated that he was born in AD 794. His father of course was Ragnar Lothbrok. Now, Ragnar had several wives while he was chieftain of Sweden and Denmark. We don't know if Ivar ever married − but it would be more likely that he didn't.

His brothers were Halfdan of the Wide Embrace, Sigurd Snake in the Eye, Ubba, Bjorn Ironside, Rathbarth, Dunyat, Agnar, Regnald, Vithserk, Erik Wind Hat, and Fridlef. He had 11 brothers and we cannot account for their sisters. This was a large family and Ivar was the most prominent among the children.

Aslaug was called a volva (Old Norse) among their people. A volva in their culture was a female shaman and they were often referred to by many different names. The term "volva" actually translates to "carrier of the wand" or "magic staff carrier." In their days a shaman whether male or female could practice sorcery and also prophecy. You can say that they were sought after for guidance since their foresight was highly valued.

In Norse mythology, these volur (plural of volva) were held in high esteem and they were believed to possess great powers. In fact, the elder god Odin himself consulted the volur as recorded in the Völuspá (transliterates to Prophecy of the Volva).

Apparently, Princess Aslaug gave a prophecy on their wedding day, which, according to Ragnar's saga, says the following:

"Three nights together, but yet apart,

Shall we bide, nor worship the gods as yet;

From my son this would save a lasting harm,

For boneless is he thou wouldst now beget."

The couple was supposed to hold back from consummating their marriage for three days or else a curse would befall their child. The curse as Aslaug foretells is a "bonelessness." However, Ragnar got drunk and stumbled upon his newly betrothed wife. His lust got the better of him and he raped the princess right then and there.

Some sources say that Ragnar didn't believe the prophecy and so the couple consummated the marriage anyway. Whether he forced himself on his newly wed woman or the princess gave herself to him without objection, the result is still the same. The sagas continue and state that the result of that untimely union was Ivar who according to one legend was born without bones.

The sagas state the following:

"only the like of gristle where his bones should have been"

Of course we can infer or deduce what the authors were trying to describe.

Controversy over the "Boneless" Nickname

Even Ivar's nick name "The Boneless" is a matter of controversy. Before going over the many different theories about what this curious moniker means we should mention here that the Vikings were rather creative in this regard. Well, they can be but at other times they were simply crass when they created them for their countrymen.

So, why use nicknames?

Augustana College's (Illinois) very own Paul Peterson explains that surnames weren't a well-established practice during such times when the Vikings roamed the seas and ravaged kingdoms. Of course, there were many Olafs and there were plenty of Astrids who varied in physical features and bloodlines. Of course there were other Ivars who had been around.

So, how do you recognize which Olaf is which, which Astrid is which, and which Ivar is which? You go by the nickname. In the times leading to the great Viking era, epithets became quite popular or actually a more prevalent way of identifying which person you were referring to. And it would appear that the historical figures in Viking history were given the more quirky nicknames.

Peterson says that the huge number of nicknames that you can find in the literature of Old Norse is incomparably rich. He also says that the recurrence of these nicknames helps us understand the transmission of the Viking sagas as well. They teach us about the etymology of the words of the language of these people. They also reveal to us different slangs they used as well as their cultural history. He also makes it a point to elaborate that some of these nick names are just puns that the Vikings threw at each other – some of them are just downright silly.

However, do take note that Peterson also specifically points out that monarchial nicknames, this includes legendary heroes to actual historical figures such as Ivar, that these nick names are especially descriptive. Most of the time when a nickname survives all the way into Norse canon, an explanation of the epithet also helps to contextualize the monarch or royalty being discussed or described.

For example, there was a Viking war lord by the name of Óttarr the Vendel Crow. He was slain at the Battle of Vendill and it was said that his remains were eaten by crows – thus his epithet.

Another example is a Viking count by the name of Walking-Hrólfr. So why did Hrólfr walk instead of riding a horse when he was royalty? The answer is that he was a really large man that horses and beasts of burden couldn't carry him – thus, even though it was peculiar for any royalty or monarch amongst these people, Hrólfr just walked wherever he went.

There was also a Scandinavian king by the name of Magnús who was given the nickname Barelegged. So, why were this king's legs bare? King Magnus traveled and raided in the British Isles and he and his men adopted the kilts that the men there wore – thus their legs were left unprotected without armor on. He brought this seemingly odd fashion statement back to Norway when he came back but alas fortune tells that he died after his bared leg was wounded by an enemy.

Due take note that sometimes the explanations of the nicknames of non-royal Vikings may also be included in the recorded text. That means that it doesn't follow that all Viking nick names that had explanations of them were automatically of royal descent and that those without explanation weren't. The presence of an explanation of these nick names in the annals doesn't guarantee royal lineage.

So, what about Ivar the Boneless?

As it turns out, there is no direct or solid explanation as to Ivar's nickname. Yet we should note that he was definitely of royal descent. He was one of the princes of the land ruled by his father Ragnar Lothbrok. On top of that, Ivar was the first born son, which meant that he was regarded as heir to his father's throne.

And yet, in spite of his status there is no clear explanation as to his epithet, which is quite a curiosity. In fact, scholars have debated the strange nick name given to such a cunning and brutal warrior. There are a lot of theories as to the real meaning behind his name. Let's go over most known of them.

Theory #1 – Boneless Means that Ivar was a Cripple

Even though it isn't clear where the "Boneless" epithet came from, the sagas themselves describe the man Ivar to be a person who is lacking in bones. Of course that sort of description is open to varying interpretations.

However, there are those who believe that it is possible that Ivar the Boneless was a cripple. If you base things according to his birth and origins in the sagas already mentioned earlier, then we may conclude that Ivar was a cripple.

There is contention among scholars as to whether Ivar the Boneless did suffer from a genetic disease that crippled him for life or not. We'll cover the details about that in the next chapter.

Theory #2 – That Ivar Was Impotent

Another theory is that the "boneless" moniker meant that Ivar was impotent and unable to produce children. This also has roots in the sagas, which say that the man had *"neither love nor lust played any part in his life."* That might explain why such a ferocious Viking leader would leave behind no posterity to call after his name.

Theory #3 – The Family Tradition of Snakes and Serpents

Another theory that people use to try to explain the rather peculiar epithet is that tradition of having serpents in their family to show prowess and other worthy qualities and slyness. Ivar's father Ragnar is said to have slayed a giant serpent for instance. His brother Sigurd is nick named Snake in the Eye – which may infer a medical/physical condition concerning the eyes or that he has pretty good vision, and of course finally Ivar's being "boneless," which can possibly be attributed to a certain level of flexibility.

Theory #4 – Ivar was Flexible in Bed

Speaking of flexibility, this is another explanation that bases itself in the sagas again. This time from the Flateyjarbók, a book or record that dates back to 1387 (according to internal evidence – completed in 1394). The bonelessness of Ivar describes how he was when he ravished women, very flexible and very serpent-like, which ties back to the previous theory. Again, do take note that this saga was written several hundred years after the events.

Theory #5 – His Moniker Meant the Exact Opposite

As it was stated earlier, nicknames do tend to be silly and at times they mean exactly the opposite of the feature they are describing. We know sometimes that people label someone who is absolutely enormous as "tiny" or maybe another ironic Viking nickname that we can use as an example is "lofty" referring to such a man who was actually pretty short. Some of the descriptions of Ivar was that he was very tall usually anywhere from 7 to 9 feet tall. If there was such a Viking with that kind of stature, then the Nordic folks of the day would be pretty keen at using irony to call him "boneless" in spite of the fact that he had really big bones – and that fits the milieu perfectly.

Theory #6 – Boneless Means "The Hated"

There is this other theory that the moniker boneless means that Ivar was hated or the hated one. This is a bit of a scholarly theory though since it draws from the Latin Exosus. The theory goes that a medieval scribe could have misinterpreted the writing and transcribed it differently from "the hated" to "the boneless" (i.e. ex + os or without + bones instead of exosus which means "the hated"). However, this theory is difficult to square when you move away from Latin sources and go back to the original Norse manuscripts that record his name as "the boneless" and not as "the hated."

Theory #7 – Boneless Means "The Ruthless"

Yet another explanation about Ivar's name is drawn from the Old Norse *Beinlausi* which of course transliterates to "boneless" in English. However, an alternate translation of this word is "ruthless." Someone who has been given this name will be one without ethics or morals as well as sexual restraints.

Unfortunately the exact account of Ivar's origins is actually unknown to us. Even the extant meaning of his epithet is very hard to decipher since the sagas have been interlaced with folklore. We can entertain and perhaps analyze the different theories that explain the meaning of his name but we can never really come to anything conclusive given the material and sources that we currently have.

Controversy about Ivar's Disability

"What's in a name? That which we call a rose by any other name would smell as sweet."

–William Shakespeare

Osteogenesis Imperfecta

Some people suggest that Ivar the Boneless suffered from a genetic bone disease known as osteogenesis imperfecta – otherwise known as brittle bone disease. This disease can cause a person to have an imperfect bone formation. That means the one suffering from this medical condition can make their joints bend off far beyond the usual limits.

In the previous chapter we have the backdrop provided by the sagas about Ivar suffering a physical disability from birth due to a curse that was prophesied by his mother, Aslaug.

However, do take note that there are different cases of this disease. The effects of this condition ranges from tolerable (which means the one suffering from it can still lead a productive life) to effects that are completely life threatening. There are those who have this condition who are confined for life on a wheelchair but could still join Paralympic games. However, there are those who would always be in constant threat of injury. For instance those who have very brittle bones could crack a rib or dislocate an arm when they have severe coughing fits.

Now, if Ivar the Boneless was such a cripple then he must have been quite extraordinary. Of course, there are plenty of experts on medieval and ancient history who would frown at the suggested idea of a Viking warlord who led the greatest army of Danes but couldn't even walk.

Although of course there have been ancient rulers and generals who were otherwise disabled who also led their troops to battle and gained the respect of their soldiers. One good example of which is

Agesilaus, who lived centuries before Ivar. Just like Ivar, Agesilaus should have been discarded as a babe with deformities because the same custom was followed in Sparta during the 5th century.

Agesilaus was half-brother to the king, a prince just like Ivar. He was allowed to live and eventually became king. Another example of royalty surviving such odds is Claudius of Rome. He had a speech impediment from birth so much so that everyone regarded him as being feeble minded. Eventually Claudius eventually became emperor of Rome.

Now, it should also be pointed out that Ivar was no less than a prince – he was royalty. If indeed he was a cripple then the people would have respected his bloodline not to mention the fact that he was a brilliant strategist.

Ivar would have been a charismatic fellow who could inspire men to believe in him and do his will. They would trust him because he has led them to war providing tactics that beat the enemy time and again. In some cultures he could have been thought of being special or someone who was blessed – and to some extreme he would have been worshipped.

However, here again the sagas and records would seem to contradict their own accounts. Well, on the one hand we have a prince and a warlord who is described as someone who couldn't walk. He was even described as being quite skilled with a long bow – which fit the conditions perfectly. Yes, even a man suffering from brittle bones disease can still fire a long bow effectively and be good at it. In spite of that, there are parts of the record that say that Ivar was a berserker.

In one rendering of the story of Ivar the Boneless, Ivar was one of the biggest berserkers around. In fact, he led an elite team of berserkers when he attacked Dublin, Ireland. Now that is hardly a man whom you could brand as a cripple.

Now this is one of the more confusing part of his history. We clearly do not have anything definitive that would clarify the meaning of his epithet. In fact, in one part of the annals, the record directly contradicts itself – take this one for example:

"Only cartilage was where bone should have been , but otherwise he grew tall and handsome and in wisdom he was the best of their children."

Now, if there was only cartilage in his body where there should have been any bone then how in the world was Ivar the Boneless able to stand? And how else could he grow tall (perhaps taller than most kids in his day)? In spite of his being "boneless" he was the best of the royal children and he was more handsome and wise to boot.

We can attribute these descriptions to literary license by the bard or poet who wrote the verse but maybe there is a kernel of truth to it. Could Ivar have been quite a persuasive person, the smartest of Ragnar's children, and a truly charismatic leader? Well, we could just throw in the good looks part for good measure if you want.

Another interesting detail that can be used by proponents of the idea that Ivar was a cripple is the fact that the legends say that he was carried by his men on shields or on a shield during battle. The stories say that he would urge his warriors to do their best and his men would be inspired and become truly violent on the field of battle. Ivar himself would lead them and since he couldn't walk he would be borne by a troop of his men on a shield – and perhaps there he would fire away with his bow.

Being held up high allows a tactician to survey the opposing army's position. If he used the terrain to his advantage, he could use the height advantage to snipe select targets – like commanders on the field.

With the matter of war leaders being carried about on shields, the records also become a bit confusing. According to one chronicler of the time, Geoffrey of Wells, it was not Ivar that was carried by his troops on their shields but it was Ubba his half-brother. The chronicler even attributed devilish powers to Ivar's brother, which gave them the advantage over any opposing army. The chronicler specifically states that Ubba was raised high to gaze at the enemy forces.

The sagas state that it was Ivar who was raised on shields but a contemporary recorder says it was his brother. Could Geoffrey of Wells have mistaken Ubba for Ivar? Unfortunately, we would never know.

This would have been quite plausible. However, we also learn from other experts that it is a tradition among the Vikings for their commanders to be borne on shields resting on the shoulders of their men. This tradition is done whether you're a cripple or not. Was Ivar really a cripple? Was he raised up high for strategic purposes? We may never really know for sure.

Professor Biddle and His 9 Foot Tall Viking

Perhaps the biggest contention against the theory that Ivar the Boneless had a physical disability comes from archaeology. The husband and wife team of Professor Martin Biddle and his wife Birthe Biddle of Oxford University have presented a powerfully compelling case against the theory.

In their excavations they have come across a truly peculiar Norse grave site in Repton's the churchyard of St Wystan. At the center of the mass grave are the remains of a 9 foot tall Viking warrior. This humongous Viking that was excavated in southern Derbyshire is believed to be none other than Ivar the Boneless.

Scandinavians who are 9 feet tall are of course a rarity. Consider the living conditions that they had and the fact that they really had a problem producing food (usually the crops that they produce can only be sufficient for one family only). That would mean you won't see a lot of really tall Vikings.

Note that the sagas also mentioned Ivar's stature that it was comparatively larger than that of his contemporaries. He would usually carry a more powerful bow and he would usually use heavier arrows. The stories emphasize that he dwarfed his fighting companions. If that were so then by his sheer size, he would have intimidated any enemy and won the allegiance of his friends.

So, is the Repton giant Ivar the Boneless? Professor Martin Biddle believes he is. One important point that he brings up is that the histories records that the Great Heathen Army actually traveled to Repton back in 873 AD. This was at the close of the illustrious career of Ivar Ragnarsson.

They made their winter quarters there in that year but before they moved on they left a mass grave on the site. Now this was no ordinary Viking – he was a rather important ruler or leader of the band. You can tell because the grave itself that they constructed for this man was special. It was no ordinary grave and deposited in it was no ordinary Viking.

The grave that Professor Biddle and his wife dug was no less than a huge mess. Professor Biddle explains that he and his team weren't the first ones to dig out the site. Apparently a worker or grave digger by the name of Thomas Walker dug up the mass burial place back in 1686.

He disturbed the arrangement of the bones since he didn't understand what he discovered. However he took copious notes of the discovery and documented the dig site. He described in detail the things that he dug up.

The giant of a Viking that they dug up was from 35 to 45 years of age. He must have been a very important Viking warlord due to several factors. Surrounding him in his burial site were at least 249 bodies. He was buried with a boar's tusk, a small Thor's hammer and a sword. These according to Viking belief will be with him when he crosses over to Valhalla.

After examination, Professor Biddle concludes that the said Viking warlord died a brutal death. He was stabbed in the head twice, probably by spears. Evidence of which is the pair of wounds on the giant's skull. A spinal injury on the said body showed that he might have been disemboweled as well.

So, why the boar tusk? According to the Viking religion no one will be accepted into Valhalla if one's body was not whole. Evidence suggests that the Repton giant was castrated and his genitals have been removed. This Viking received injuries in the head, arm, jaw, and the thigh. The boar's tusk was an effort by his compatriots to restore his body to wholeness thus allowing him entry into Valhalla – the tusk was found in between his legs.

Why was this man discmboweled and all the agonizing injuries wrought upon him? One expert from Manchester University, Dr. Bob Stoddart, suggests that his brutal death was a result of a revenge attack since the Vikings destroyed the church at Repton along with the monastery adjoining the church building.

Experts argue that there was no other important Viking warlord at the time and at the same place other than Ivar the Boneless. Part of the annals that describe Ivar match that of the towering giant that they have unearthed; and thus Professor Biddle and his team present a powerful case. However, do take note that even though their case can be quite convincing it is not conclusive. The evidence suggest that this was an important Viking but there is no 100% solid proof that this was the very Ivar of legend.

Ivar's Family

"You don't choose your family. They are God's gift to you, as you are to them."

—Desmond Tutu

Ivar the Boneless comes from quite a reputable family in Viking terms that is. You can say that his family was truly legendary. With a parentage like Ragnar Lothbrok and Aslaug plus a huge number of brothers who made a name, fame, and notoriety for themselves, you can say that Ivar was truly in good company. You can even say that their family is truly includes some of the who's who in Viking history.

In this chapter we will touch on Ivar's rather legendary family line.

Ragnar Lothbrok

Since the record of Ivar's birth is mentioned, with details provided for, in the saga of Ragnar Lothbrok then it should only be proper to become acquainted with the man who fathered such an infamous child. His name is spelled in several ways. His first name can be spelled as Ragnar or Ragnarr. His other name is either rendered as Lothbrok or Lodbrok. Nevertheless, however it is spelled we are of course referring to the one and the same person.

The name Lothbrok or Lodbrok means hairy breeches or shaggy breeches. Why did he wear hairy pants? It was said that he wore them during the time when he betrothed his first wife and the nickname clung almost instantly. Ragnar is of both Swedish and Danish descent. He is also both a Viking ruler and also a hero according to the sagas and poetry in Old Norse. According to this same Viking literature Ragnar became quite a distinguished fellow because of his raids in England and France.

There are those of course who question whether Ragnar Lothbrok ever did exist or is he just a legendary figure that can only be as real as the mythic sagas that talk about him. There are significant records that mention him although historians will argue whether or not it is the Ragnar Lothbrok of the sagas or some other person who may also have the same name.

Some of the sources that we can draw from to ascertain Ragnar's existence includes the following:

Krákumál – "Ragnar's Death-Song" which is a 12th-century Scottish skaldic poem.

Ragnarsdrápa – a poem by the skalds which is attributed to a 9th-century poet by the name of Bragi Boddason. There are many existing fragments of this poem.

Völsunga saga – a legendary Icelandic saga that dates back to the 13th century. This long prose tells of the wars and succession of kings that ultimately lead to the birth and kingship of Ragnar Lothbrok.

Tale of Ragnar Lothbrok – this is another legendary saga and it is sequel to the Völsunga saga.

Ragnarssona þáttr – "Tale of Ragnar's Sons," this is another saga but this one covers the deeds of Ragnar's sons after his death. This mentions the conquest of English lands by Ivar and his brothers.

Gesta Danorum Book IX – A record by Saxo Grammaticus, a Christian Danish chronicler. This record history dates back to the 12th century.

The extent of Ragnar's historicity isn't absolutely clear since his life is only recorded partially in different written sources. Even in the historical record written by Saxo Grammaticus, we will only find fragmentary information because his work is more of an effort to consolidate the many events about Ragnar's life that at times are both confusing and contradictory – this according to Hilda Davidson.

The biggest achievement that we can attribute to Ragnar Lothbrok was the Siege of Paris which eventually culminated in the Sack of

Paris in the year 845. According to Frankish accounts in the 9th century, the Viking force that attacked Paris was led by none other than Ragnar Lothbrok, although again as stated earlier, the identification of Ragnar as leader is disputed by scholars and historians alike.

The Sack of Paris was actually the culmination of a series of events. Ragnar was given land in Turholt by Charles the Bald himself. However, Ragnar lost the favor of the king and the land was taken as well. In response, Ragnar invaded taking advantage of their maneuverability along the Seine River. King Charles assembled an army which he divided into two divisions split on the two sides of the river.

Ragnar attacked and defeated the smaller division of the Frankish army. 111 prisoners were taken and later hanged on a small island along the Seine River to incite terror amongst the Frankish troops and as an offering to the war god Odin.

Ragnar met his death in 865 AD under the hands of King Ælla of Northumbria. His death instigated his sons to exact revenge and resulted in the formation of the Great Heathen Army. The exploits of this army as led by Ivar the Boneless will be covered in a later chapter.

Queen Aslaug

Queen Aslaug is another mythical figure in the legends of the north. Her name is also rendered in a variety of ways such as Aslog. She is also called Kraka or Kraba, which translates to "crow" from Old Norse. In the saga of Ragnar Lothbrok she is recorded as the third wife. In other records she is the second wife, this is again another part of the sagas that appear conflicting as well as confusing.

She was the daughter of Sigurd and Brynhildr, the shieldmaiden, which gives her royal descent. However, at the death of her parents, she was raised by her foster grandfather by the name of Heimer. At the death of Aslaug's parents, Heimer became concerned for the safety of his granddaughter.

To provide protection and avoid trouble, Heimer posed as a poor harp player constructing a rather large harp. In the body of the harp he hid Aslaug. He needed to conceal the girl because her really attractive beauty betrays her royal origin. He traveled and played the harp for money all the while hiding Aslaug in the harp.

One day they traveled to Spangereid in Norway and they stayed in the home of peasants by the name of Ake and Gima. Ake believed that the harp that Heimer was carrying contained valuable treasures. He then conspired with his wife and later that night killed Heimer in his sleep.

When they opened the large harp they found Aslaug inside it. They then raised the girl as their own child and gave her the name Kraka, which meant crow in their native language. Of course they now have the burden to hide the obvious signs of her noble birth, her beauty. What the couple did is to rub tar on the girl and dress her in a long hood.

Years went by and as the maiden grew, she was discovered by the men of Ragnar Lothbrok as she was bathing. Her beauty amazed the men who having been mesmerized left their bread to burn. Ragnar then inquired why had they left the bread to burn and the men described the maiden that had entranced them.

Ragnar then sent her an invitation but he tested her wits. He sent for her but told that she should come dressed and undressed and that she should also she should not be fasting or eating. He also said that she should also come over alone and with company.

Aslaug arrived wearing a net for clothes. She also came biting an onion and for a companion she had a dog. Ragnar was impressed by her wits and beauty and he proposed marriage to her. She of course refused until his mission in Norway has been fulfilled. She also gave a prophecy and a curse that if she and her new husband would consummate their marriage before three days-time that their first born son would be "boneless."

Of course, as stated in an earlier chapter of this book, Ragnar raped her in a drunken fit and their first born son became Ivar and he had that bonelessness that was prophesied by Aslaug. She bore Ragnar four children who were Ivar, Hvitserk, Ubba, and Sigurd.

Björn Ironside

Björn Ironside is another legendary king among the north men and he is the first king of the Munso Dynasty. The annals and legends also get confusing when it comes to Björn's lineage. In one saga he is the son of Ragnar and Aslaug, which can be found in the Ragnarssona þáttr (i.e. Tale of Ragnar's Sons). However, in other accounts it is recorded that he is the son of Ragnar and Thora, supposedly Ragnar's third wife which is also another confusing part of the sagas.

In Old Norse his name is rendered as Bjǫrn Járnsíða. His name in Icelandic is rendered as Björn Járnsíða but in Swedish it is Björn Järnsida. In his native Danish his name is Bjørn Jernside but among the Latin speaking nations where he conquered he was known as Bier Costae ferreae. The date of his birth is unknown so we can just affix it as sometime within the 9th century.

Before succeeding his father as king of Norway, he led many excursions into France and England often accompanied by Hastein. The identity of Hastein is also another point of confusion. In some of the records he is the brother of Björn Ironside while in others he is the mentor and close friend of his father Ragnar. Nevertheless, brother or mentor, he and Björn traveled and fought together.

In the year 860 Björn brought with him a huge expeditionary force to the Mediterranean for raiding. They raided along the Iberian coast all the way to Gibraltar. From there they raided the southern regions of France.

After the winter that year they landed in Italy and finally captured the city of Pisa. Believing that they were headed to Rome, they looted the town of Luni. However, they were not able to breach the town's walls.

They then devised a plan where they tricked the local bishop into believing that one of the raiding Viking leaders, Hastein, was near death and wanted to make a death bed conversion to Christianity and be buried on consecrated ground, supposedly within the church grounds.

The bishop couldn't refuse the request for a man who wanted to receive Christian sacraments. They then let Hastein in – he was on a stretcher appearing to be near death. They let him in with a small honor guard. However, after getting into the church, Hastein leaped off of his bed and with his men hacked their way to the gates. They then opened the gates and let the rest of their raiders in.

Björn and Hastein met a terrific defeat after a series of successful raids in North Africa and Sicily. They were carrying their spoils on their ships as they headed back to Gibraltar. They were met by Al-Andalus ships along the way and a fierce sea battle enraged. Björn lost 40 of his best ships at that time. The enemy used what was referred to as Greek fire, which was very effective at the time. However, Björn was able to escape and return Scandinavia as a hero and ruled the country. He lived the rest of his life as a rich man.

Halfdan Ragnarsson

Halfdan is another Viking leader of the Great Heathen Army and brother to Ivar the Boneless. He was there when the great army invaded the Anglo Saxon kingdoms in 865 AD. He was also the first crowned Viking kings of Northumbria.

It is said that when they invaded, they were identified as the Danes, which meant that they were men of Denmark. However, it would seem that the English chroniclers did get confused sometimes as they made their hasty records since they were frequently on the run from the invading forces. One chronicler and churchman by the name of Asser put on record that the invaders were de Danubia or from the Danube, which is pretty far from the actual origin of the invading army. What he might have really meant was that the invaders were de Dania which literally meant as Denmark.

Halfdan was part of the army that crushed the Northumbrians that eventually led to the brutal torture and execution of King Ælla. Other than his participation in the Great Army, Halfdan also laid claim to the kingship of Dublin. However, he died in 877 in what was known as the Battle of Strangford Lough, where he was pressing his claim to the throne.

Did Halfdan really exist? According to scholar Hilda Ellis Davidson, part of the narrative of the English invasion of the Danes is based on historical fact. That means Halfdan along with Ivar and the rest of the Ragnarsson brothers were in fact historical figures. Remember that Halfdan is sometimes regarded as the second brother in the family after Ivar.

Hvitserk

Hvitserk or Vithserk actually means "white shirt" if transliterated from the original language of the Vikings. There is no dispute as to whether he was a brother of Ivar the Boneless or not. However, there is a bit of confusion with regard to his parentage. In some records his mother was no other than Aslaug. However, there are also records where he was the 9th brother of Ivar and his mother was Svanloga, Ragnar Lothbrok's fourth wife. Again, there is no way that we can ascertain which is true and which isn't at this point.

Hvitserk came with his brother Ivar to the English shores to avenge the death of his father Ragnar Lothbrok. However, scholars are at odds as to who he is and if he really did come with his brothers to England. For instance, there are no records other than the Ragnarssona þáttr that mentions Hvitserk fighting alongside his brother Halfdan Ragnarsson, who was clearly one of the leaders of the Great Heathen Army. This has led some scholars to believe that Hvitserk and Halfdan were one and the same man with Hvitserk being only a nickname. Of course, that theory is also another matter of debate since you can also draw his existence from other sources that details the family of Ragnar Lothbrok.

Unfortunately not much is known about Hvitserk. It is said in the annals and sagas that after avenging their father's death that he traveled to Garðaríki and raided there. He and his men particularly attacked and raided with the Rus. Unfortunately, his army was defeated and he was reportedly burned at a stake alive along with other human remains.

Sigurd Snake-in-the-Eye

Sigurd's name in Old Norse is rendered as Sigurðr ormr í auga. He was a Viking warrior and son of Ragnar Lothbrok. Together with Ivar the Boneless and their other brothers, they invaded Anglo Saxon England to avenge the death of their father.

His nick name "snake in the eye" denotes a physical anomaly about his eyes. It is said that he was born with a mark in his eye in the shape of a snake. In other records this mark is said to be in the form of a snake that is biting its own tail – an Ouroboros. This snake mark in his eye is partly folklore since the sagas mention that this mark was prophesied by his mother Aslaug who was a volg. This prophecy was part of her mother's proof to her husband that she was of noble birth.

It is also said that Sigurd had a special close relationship with his father Ragnar. Some have said that he accompanied the Viking king in an expedition to Hellespont, Russia. However, that claim still needs to be verified. It is also said that Sigurd also undertook a journey to the Scottish islands.

When his father died, the Viken, Danish islands, Halland, Scania, and Zealand were given to him as an inheritance. In 877 he succeeded in the kingship of Denmark after his brother Halfdan Ragnarsson died. Strange enough, there are records that indicate that Sigurd married king Ælla's daughter (the very king who had his father killed). Her name was Blaeja and she bore him four children.

Ubba

Ubba is one of the primary commanders of the Great Heathen Army along with Ivar the Boneless, of course. Ubba is also known as Ubbi, Ubbe, or Hubba. Ubba himself was a Viking chieftan in their native land. Now, his being son to Ragnar Lothbrok is also suspected by historians today. The connection of Ubba to Ragnar is disputed just as much as the historicity of Ragnar his father.

Part of the confusion comes from the fact that part of the English sources of the record also state that a portion of the invading heathen army is from Frisia and one of these contemporary records say that the Ubba that accompanied the heathen army that invaded

Wessex, East Anglia, Mercia, and Northumbria was the dux or leader of the Frisians. Again, this is another part of the records both contemporary and saga that conflicts one another. Well, at least we know for sure that there was an Ubba that invaded ancient England with Ivar the Boneless in 865 AD and so forth.

Part of the records associates Ubba with the death of St. Edmund, the king of the East Angles. They say that Ivar and Ubba were the main spirits who ushered the ultimate death of the king. However, there are near contemporary records that do not make this connection with Ivar. Further evidence of this disassociation is in the fact that after the death of King Edmund, Ivar left the command of the Great Heathen Army to Halfdan and not to Ubba.

However, if we trace the records of Ubba's death in 878, it is said that the site of his death was in Wind Hill in Devon near the Countisbury. It was said that this was the site of the defeat of the remnants of the Viking army that Ivar brought across the seas. It is quite ironic that their end was met at the hands of local men. Medieval sources state was the final leader of this band of Vikings was none other than Ubba and he was numbered among those who were slain in this final battle.

In previous chapter we mentioned that there were a lot more sons of Ragnar Lothbrok. However, since the information about them is rather scarce and they were rarely mentioned in the annals of the Great Heathen Army that fought alongside Ivar the Boneless then their details have been excluded.

Ivar the Viking

"What is interesting to me about Vikings is that they were failed farmers."

–Roger Avary

So what was Ivar the Boneless like? It wouldn't be hard to imagine him to be a man who commands the respect of a horde of killers. That would mean that he is a truly fearsome human being whom wouldn't be to pleasant to meet face to face.

It is a fact that the Vikings of the 9th century have been getting a lot of press for quite a while. When we say Viking a lot of the stereotypes that have been cast about them in popular media will be the first things to come to mind. Can you spell Thor from the Marvel Cinematic Universe? It wouldn't be that hard to spot and it wouldn't need any elaboration that when we describe Ivar as a Viking then we would imagine him to be quite a shaggy muscle bound character with maybe a pair of wooden legs to boot. There is no need to point out that these stereotypes are hardly accurate.

Typical Stereotypes If Ivar was Cast into the Modern Mold

A good example of the usual stereotype can be found in the animated movie ***How to Train Your Dragon (2010)***. Here we have a protagonist, Hiccup, who is a rather scrawny kid compared to his tough and war-like kinsmen – not to mention his buff and tough father.

Another example of such stereotype is ***The 13th Warrior (1999)*** movie, which stars Antonio Banderas, directed by Michael Crichton. Banderas was the rather mild mannered but highly intelligent Arab surrounded by big strong and rough Viking men. Of course the costumes were crafted quite nicely and the burial by boat was a bit accurate. Also, the fact that the Vikings in this movie consulted a volg or seer woman is another aspect of Viking culture that we can say is a bit accurate as well.

Another example of an effort to cast a more accurate account of Viking life and culture is from the 2005 movie entitled ***Beowulf and Grendel*** which is of course drawn from another saga not exactly related to Ivar the Boneless or his father Ragnar, but the movie does give us a glimpse of their culture.

Perhaps one of the currently more popular efforts to portray the lives of these seafaring Vikings are two TV series – ***The Last Kingdom*** and ***Vikings***. The Vikings TV series produced by the History Channel cover Ragnar's exploits which includes the sacking of Paris and the later wars fought by his sons. The Last Kingdom is some sort of an aftermath tale after the wars fought by the Great Heathen Army that avenged Ragnar's death. These TV series are good efforts but it can't be denied that they still might fall a bit short of portraying 9th century Viking life exactly as it really were.

Of course, some of movie and TV portrayals are just way too ahistorical. A good example of such a film is the 1950s movie ***The Vikings,*** which starred Tony Curtis who donned a leather jerkin that skimmed a little too much buttocks.

These movies and television series portray Norway and Denmark as lands overflowing with horned helmet donning blood thirsty killers and warriors. Part of the stereotype is that these Vikings were more into rowing their long ships, killing and murdering, destroying monasteries, ax throwing contests, working themselves into berserker rages, and of course ravishing virgins. These of course are undeniably part of what Vikings actually did during their raids but that doesn't paint a complete picture of these people.

Information Rehabilitation

It should be noted also that a lot of information rehabilitation has been going on since the early 60s. Scholars and historians have been working hard in correcting the inconsistencies and false portrayals of these Vikings in popular media and there are media producers who have been pretty keen at listening to them.

For instance, we now know that we ought to be grateful to these Vikings because they were responsible for producing the Lewis Chessmen. Now, we can also give credence to History Channel's TV series Vikings – it's quite popular and it receives consistent high ratings–since it does show that these seafaring warriors did play a form of chess and they produced chessmen carved out of wood. Ivar himself is cast playing the game to show how much a strategist he was.

Some of the corrective measures include informing the general public that these Vikings are more of farmers, settlers, and traders – well, apart from being rapists and killers of course. We shouldn't fail to also mention that these people are also active in human trafficking. The slave trade was as much a huge part of their lives as handling the plow and pitchfork and fishing – this according to medievalist Jonathan Jarrett. A lot of these Vikings got really rich by participating in the slave trade.

It might even surprise you to know that Vikings may be a bit more into grooming compared to the English folks with whom they fought against. For instance, Vikings carried ear spoons to remove excess ear wax and they bathed more often than their Angle, Saxon, Mercian, and other opponents. This is according to a campaign launched by the University of Cambridge. On top of that, it is said that these Vikings eventually joined with the property owning classes of the very folks they invaded, according to archaeologist Francis Pryor.

So, was Ivar that peace loving farmer who just happened to have a hobby of slaughtering people, raping women, and pillaging villages and cities or is it another thing? He wouldn't be hailed as the leader of the greatest army of Danes ever raised since time memorial if the people didn't believe in Ivar's overall ferocity, fighting skills, and war tactics, right? What you will find in the following are tidbits that might help cast a clearer picture of an Ivar the Boneless of the 9th century.

Ivar Never Wore a Horned Helmet

Did Ivar the Boneless wear a horned Viking hat? That's the most Viking thing that one can ever do, right? Wrong. If you would like to get to know the historical Vikings of Midgard then you should forget all the Viking costumes that you have ever seen on TV. Ivar wouldn't have worn a helmet with horns on it.

Of course he would have worn some type of head gear. You wouldn't last long against volleys of arrows without something to protect your head. Depictions that were drawn during the Viking age do not show them wearing horned helmets and there is one actual archaeological specimen of such a helmet but alas it doesn't have any horns – nor does it hint that it used to have any.

Ivar would have worn the usual helmet to cover his head. So where did the horns come from? There are those who believe that the horns are from depictions by Roman as well as Greek chroniclers, which aren't exactly accurate. However, it should be noted that it was the Norse priests who wore the horned helmets when officiating in their religious ceremonies and not the seafaring Viking warriors.

Ivar the Boneless Is Very Hygienic for His Age

There were no showers in the 9th century obviously. And due to the cold climate, the people in the world in those days bathed less frequently. By less frequently we should make it clear that that meant not bathing in weeks. People would just throw on new clothes and spray some perfume on, if they could afford it.

Ivar and the rest of his crew would have been a lot better. They would bathe at least once a week, which is already far better than their medieval counterparts. He and his men would be carrying grooming tools made from antlers such as ear cleaners, combs, razors, and tweezers.

These men were warriors, yes, but they liked to be groomed and dressed well for battle. Of course, they couldn't take a dip when they were traveling across the seas for months but they did enjoy bathing in natural hot springs whenever there was occasion for one. So don't be surprised to find out that Ivar the Boneless to be the equivalent of a 9th century James Bond type of character – elegant but deadly.

That Liquid Fire Starter

Vikings were practical folk, which means they would not shy away from using anything and everything to survive in the harsh environments that they found themselves in. Starting a fire is one skill that you can't live without in the 8th or 9th century. Well, they didn't have matches back then so they resorted to the next best material that they can use – human urine. Say that again?

Vikings like Ivar the Boneless wouldn't have any qualms about using that sort of liquid to start fires. The technology they used is really simple actually. They usually collect a fungus from tree barks which they called touch wood.

This fungus would be boiled in human urine for several days. They would have to start a fire every night and so they did. The sodium nitrate in urine makes the touch wood smolder instead of burning. That means these guys could take fire with them whilst on the go – it's a pretty smart move. Would Ivar know such a technology? You bet he would.

Burial Boats

If you have seen the Lord of the Rings movie series, or if you have read the books (specifically JRR Tolkien's The Two Towers) you would know that people buried their dead on boats. In the Lord of the Rings one such character that was buried in a boat that was cast adrift in the river was Boromir.

On the boat you would find the warrior's weapons and a lot of different trinkets which would include the weapons of the enemies that he has defeated. They would even shoot a fiery arrow at the boat to burn it as it floated away.

It shouldn't come as a surprise that this burial by boat ritual is very Viking indeed. Among those who believe in the Norse religion, the valiant warrior is given a rather glorious and festive welcome in the halls of Valhalla. It is also believed that the traveling vessels (i.e. their ships) would serve them well as transports in the afterlife. This special treatment isn't for distinguished warriors alone.

Prominent community figures, that would include men and women, also get buried by boat as a special honor. It wouldn't be that difficult to think that when Ivar or any of his commanders died, they would have buried them via boat or practiced some special burial method. Their bodies would be surrounded or at least have one weapon most likely their sword. Their corpse would also be adorned with valuable goods. It wouldn't be uncommon to have the honored dead's body to be surrounded by the bodies of slaves sacrificed to the gods. Does this paint a familiar picture? Remember Professor Biddle's 9 foot giant Viking?

Getting Rich in the Slave Trade

Why did Ivar and the other Vikings go out raiding in the first place? There are several reasons why they did that. And one of the reasons why they did it is to gain riches. That would mean that they had to stole and pillage but there also were faster ways to gain riches in those days.

Of course they killed the men who opposed them in their attack. Dying a glorious death in battle is a sure fire way to get into Valhalla, or so we are told by Norse mythology. However, what do you do with the women and the younger men who were left behind in the coastal towns and territories that they raided?

The answer from Ivar and the other Vikings would be simple – you sell them as slaves. The many Celtic, Slavic, and Anglo-Saxon settlements along the coasts provided a good source of slaves – or "thralls" as they would have called them. Where were these slaves sold off to? It would be interesting to note that Vikings are traders and they also traded slaves in the slave markets of the Middle East and in Europe as well.

Viking Women Rights

Ivar would have considered Viking women as equals in the battlefield. You may have heard of Valkyries, right? In Old Norse their name would be rendered as valkyrja, which translates to "selector of the slain." The curious thing about these mythical creatures is that they are all women. Women were actually held in high regard amongst the northern people.

It should also be noted that Viking girls usually got married at the tender age of 12. That might come as a shock to some. However, it should be noted here that the age of 12 has long been held as the common law age of marriage for girls – and it was 14 for boys. Note that even in the United States, there are states and territories where there is no set marriageable age for both boys and girls and this common law age of marriage are usually followed where there is none. So technically, in such states you can still get married when a girl turns 12, which is the statutory minimum age for girls.

Another interesting point here is that even though young women can and did get married at such a young and tender age, it did not mean that their marriage was consummated immediately. Some men would wait until their young brides were better able to bear children before getting in bed with them.

These married Viking women of course were the ones left to tend to the house and the rest of the property while the men and the boys were out on their long boats having adventures. Unlike the other medieval women in Europe, Viking women had a lot of freedom.

Well, they didn't have to go out on women's movements to get those rights – their society already accepted them as having such. For instance, unlike the women in medieval times (and we can say until sometime in the 17th and 18th century – yes a long way from home since the 9th century, which is ironic for the women in the rest of the world), Viking women can inherit property.

Yes, these women can own the soil they tilled while their husbands were off sailing long boats for glory and fame (and of course fortune). If the bride didn't like her husband (or given any other reason or grievances), she could divorce her husband – now that is something rarely afforded to women. Remember that in the Old

Testament of the Bible it was the man who would give a letter of divorcement so he could separate from his wife and not the other way around.

An example of that would be Joseph, the supposed mortal father of Jesus the Christ, who, even though he wanted to do it in private so that he would not put Mary to shame, determined that it was best to divorce his betrothed. Except of course, Joseph was persuaded not to do so by the Angel Gabriel.

So, Viking women had the power to divorce their husbands. But that's not the only thing that they can do. They were also given the right to reclaim their marriage dowries in case the marriage did end. That meant that the woman would not be left destitute. She would have been given enough possessions to help see her along unmarried life. Now that is rather gratuitous of the laws and practices of the Vikings.

You can say that Ivar would have been more respectful of Viking women in general. Of course, circumstances would change if the woman was a thrall or slave. Those rights would have been voided. And of course, Ivar the Boneless would not have provide the same preferential treatment to European women.

Farmer Ivar?

So, what would be the one thing that Ivar the Boneless would be doing if he were back home in Denmark or maybe one of their territories in Iceland? Some would think that he would have been hatching some diabolical plan but no. Much to the disappointment of some he would have been a farmer just like most Viking men were.

Of course there were Vikings who preferred swords to scythes but they were more of the exception than the rule. We should also not discount the fact that there are also Vikings who have embraced the pirate way of life. They would stay on their ships and head for shore only to pillage and steal.

But Ivar, the prince, son of Ragnar Lothbrok, would most likely be at home and not on a ship. You might even see him tending to the flocks since they would usually raise sheep, pigs, goats, and cattle. It wouldn't also be surprising to find him in the field tending to the oats, rye, and barley. Note that they would be farming for only part of the year since they only had a brief summer. The food that they planted and produced would only be enough to provide for one family.

Ivar on Skis

In their native Scandinavia, it would usually be cold and snowy for the most part of the year. This could be part of the reason why they have invented skis (or a more primitive type of skis to be exact) as a more efficient means of transportation on the snow. The skis won't be a new thing in the hands of Ivar since his ancestors have invented and developed it about 6,000 years before he was born.

During the Viking age when Ivar would have lived, skis would have been pretty common. They would be used for transport as well as a fun recreation used by both men and women. This practice is so old among them they even have a god of skiing that they worshipped by the name of Ullr.

Ivar the Blonde not Brunette

If you were able to see the movie 13th Warrior, it wouldn't be that hard to notice the long blonde hair of the Viking protagonists there. That is definitely based on fact. Well, the Viking men had some degree of beauty ideals – but they are neither vain nor effeminate.

These fearsome seafaring men preferred to have blonde hair for two reasons. One is due to the current fashion trend in the land and the other reason is to get rid of head lice. Well, it would appear that they did it more for the latter than the former reason. They would use strong soap that can get rid of head lice but eventually turn their hair blonde. Men and women in their lands suffered from head lice infestations, which would of course require the use of strong soap.

Ivar the Tribal Chieftain

Here's another important fact and it would make Ivar quite the remarkable leader indeed. One Viking faction didn't recognize other factions. The people of Sweden, Norway, and Denmark in the 9th century weren't a unified group or country (well, countries) as we have them organized today.

So, imagine what great a feat it was for Ivar and his brothers to organize the largest fleet of ships and foray of warriors from these different tribal communities to fight for them to avenge their father. It would also show how much respect these people had for their father Ragnar. It would take a humongous effort to unite all these people.

Ivar not a Viking

Here's something tricky right here. The Vikings of the 9th century would most likely have not referred to themselves as "Vikings." Why is that? Well, because the word Viking is the word that is used to refer to all the people who went on expeditions overseas. They would be more likely say "let's go Viking" instead of calling themselves as Vikings, which would be weird amongst them.

Skinny Vikings

Part of the sagas says that Ivar towered his companions in battle. He would be the one to carry the heaviest bows and arrows in the company. He was actually stronger and larger than most Vikings of his day. If that was the case then he was truly an exceptional specimen of Nordic origin.

Why is that? Vikings were not really large or heavily muscled folks. Their relatively short and smaller stature was due to their diet. As stated earlier, in their native lands summers were short and that meant that there was hardly any time for them to grow crops.

The climatic conditions weren't congenial to farming. That means growing crops was really quite difficult back then in the 9th century.

On top of that, resources were usually scarce – that of course included food. Because of the limited food supply, the native Scandinavians grew smaller during their day. And finding a 9 foot tall Ivar, and a prince to boot, would be nothing more than a miracle.

However, since the living conditions in Viking lands were harsh, it bred them into a hardened people. You can say that in their desire to find better lives for themselves and their posterity, the Vikings set out into other lands on their long ships. Of course there were Vikings who sailed to sea lusting for material gain. However, a lot of these Vikings set out to have friendlier and more peaceful economic relations with other nations. They were as much as traders as they were warriors – Ivar the Boneless would have been a trader in his lifetime if he weren't raiding.

A Truly Brutal Man

It cannot also be denied that Ivar the Boneless was a truly brutal man. Evidence of which is in the manner of his execution of King Ælla – the blood eagle, which we will cover in detail in a later chapter. Another example of his brutality is in his execution of another king who was later named a martyr, King Edmund.

Abbo of Fleury, a French monk who lived in the 10th century wrote in his record entitled Life of St Edmund that Ivar commanded that his troops to take the kind and bind him. The king was said to have thrown down his weapons when Ivar walked in.

King Edmund was then beaten severely with clubs and was told to renounce his faith in Christ. The king wouldn't denounce his faith even after such a beating. Ivar then ordered that the king be tied to a tree. He then ordered his men to use the king's back as target practice.

The king's back was then peppered with arrows. It is said that his back looked like a porcupine's bristles. And then Ivar cut off the king's head and threw it in the nearby bushes and never buried his body.

The Formation of the Great Viking Army

"I am not afraid of an army of lions led by a sheep; I am afraid of an army of sheep led by a lion."

–Alexander the Great

When news of their father's death came the brothers were assembled to hear the words directly from emissaries from King Ælla himself. There the sons of Ragnar and were enraged except for Ivar the Boneless. He actually did what was considered the most un-Viking thing to do. He listened.

His brothers were already infuriated. Bjorn Ironside was said to be holding a spear – he gripped it so hard that he left imprints on it. Another of the brothers was playing chess in a nearby table; he on the other hand crushed a chessman (i.e. one of the chess pieces on the board) in his rage. One of the brothers ordered the messengers to be killed. But Ivar hushed them and wanted to hear the tale.

It was said that as the messengers told them how their father was thrown into a pit of snakes that the color of Ivar's face changed. He was listening to the details all the while he was hatching a plan in his mind. Little did King Ælla know that what he did was going to change his fate and shape the history of England. The world that he knew was about to come to an end.

The Great Viking Army

The annals say that it was Ragnar Lothbrok's sons who assembled and led the Great Heathen Army. However it should be pointed out that it was actually Ivar the Boneless who was the chief leader of this huge horde. But of course they wouldn't label themselves as "heathen" (it was an epithet that was applied to them by their Christian enemies). They were also called the Great Danish Army. Some would just call them the Great Viking Army.

Note that this army was a coalition of different forces that originated from Norway, Sweden, and Denmark. As stated in an earlier chapter, the Vikings were never a united people. However, in this particular case they were willing to put aside old rivalries so that they can accomplish a singular goal – to avenge the death of hero and king.

The name "Great Heathen Army" is taken from the 865 AD record known as the Anglo Saxon Chronicle. Their campaign is said to have lasted 14 years. Of course the original goal was to avenge the death of Ragnar Lothbrok.

However, the army that Ivar assembled didn't cross the great seas just to avenge someone's death – however important that man maybe. There was a second ulterior motive behind such a bold assembly of Viking warriors. An underlying reason was that they came to conquer – something that no man in their ranks has ever done before. Conquest was already in the mind of Ivar the Boneless as he listened to the account of his father's death.

Precursors to the English Invasion

There is no doubt that the Vikings have been raiding England prior to the landing of the great Viking Army. The records indicate that they have been raiding English lands as early as the 8th century.

They primarily raided monasteries and other treasure centers. The very first monastery that they raided was the one in Lindisfarne which was located on the island's northeast coast. This raid was conducted in the year 793 AD. The Anglo-Saxon Chronicle labeled the raiders as heathens.

Other raids were conducted. The same Chronicle says that in the year 840 that Æthelwulf of Wessex was defeated by these raiders at Carhampton in Somerset. It was said that a fleet of 35 Viking ships landed, which already comprised a major attack.

The Annals of St. Bertin also mentions the incident and reports that the battle lasted for three days. After Northmen had gained the victory they looted the surrounding areas and pillaged at will.

Of course this was one of the many sieges and raids that will be conducted by Vikings on these lands. Despite the initial setback, Æthelwulf was able to gain the upper hand on several occasions. The Anglo-Saxon Chronicle records other incidents of Viking raids that went on and off on different years until the 860s.

How the Vikings Crossed the Great Ocean

We all know that Vikings sailed on long boats. These are smaller boats compared to the much larger galleons that other countries used in later times. So, how were they able to cross such violent oceans? Well, they sailed most times and at times they rowed with their might. The next question is how did they navigate the ocean?

The answer may have been found by archaeologists from Greenland. It is already established that the Vikings were expert sailors in their time. They usually sail a North-South latitude across the Atlantic ocean. Studies recorded in the Proceedings of the Royal Society A Mathematical and Physical Sciences suggest that these Vikings may have been really sophisticated mariners. Researcher Balázs Bernáth in Hungary's Eötvös University says that these ancient mariners made use of more sophisticated navigational instruments.

A sun compass was found in Greenland that dates back to the 10th century. This compass was found in what used to be a Viking settlement. Researchers believe that these people used compasses like this and a sun crystal, which was described to be magic, to navigate during cloudy days. It is said that they used these devices to determine true north. Note that scientists have also found what they believe to be Viking sun stones.

The said sun compass was discovered by archaeologists in 1948 in the ruins of a Benedictine monastery. The said area was once a Viking settlement and was occupied by farmers back in the 10th century.

The said compass a half circle shape. It also had a center hole and a zigzag was engraved around its perimeter. They tested the compass but found that it was off by about one degree. That would translate to sailing for many days on the ocean in the wrong direction. Corrections should be made if we are to understand exactly how the Vikings were able to navigate the open ocean.

Other sailors navigated through the stars. That was not possible for the Vikings since they usually sailed near the Arctic Circle. Note that the sun will never set there during the summer – which is usually the high season for Viking raids.

On top of that, the Vikings performed latitude sailing. For example, they would choose the 61st latitude that ran from Norway to Greenland. They would sail a total of 2,500 kilometers.

One of the keys to their sailing mastery is location and timing. They would check their course at noon when the sun was at its highest in the sky. They used their ancient sun dial and it would cast a shadow on the plate. They would then measure using the scaling lines and find out the length of the shadow that was cast and they were then able to determine the latitude. This would then lead them to obtain what may be accurate measurements of both longitude and latitude, admits Amit Lerner from the Hebrew University of Jerusalem.

The Size of the Army

When Ragnar Lothbrok led the sack of Paris, he brought with him a fighting force of about 5,000 warriors. That in of itself was a huge force to reckon with. Of course that number is only an estimate. It is said that Ivar the Boneless and his brothers were able to assemble as much as 10,000 up to 15,000 warriors to cross the sea with them.

Historians have also argued about the actual size of the Great Viking Army. Some have given larger than life estimates while there are those who prefer to provide more conservative estimates. Pete Sawyer, a scholar and minimalist provides a smaller estimate than what was traditionally believed as the number of men that comprised the Great Army.

He and others dispute the fact that the Anglo-Saxon Chronicle made use of the term "hæþen here" from Old English to describe the Viking force that landed in 865 AD. They point out that back in 694

AD King Ine of Wessex has issued a code or law that defines how large a "here" should be. According to King Ine's code, a "here" would be a fighting force of about 35 men. If that were true then the number of men that followed Ivar the Boneless and his brothers to England were significantly reduced.

However, Richard Abels a historian, also suggests that the term "here" heretofore used was only devised to differentiate the Viking forces from the local combatants that served the crown. It should be noted that the Anglo-Saxon army men that served to defend the state from these Vikings were called the "fyrd." This too can be observed in the Anglo-Saxon Chronicle.

Some scholars estimate the numbers to be in the low thousands, while others are more generous about the total number of men. Some have estimated that a Viking long ship can only hold about 32 men and then they estimate the number of men by the number of ships that were used to cross the ocean. Remember that Bjorn Ironside lost at least 40 Viking ships in his raids in the Mediterranean and he still had enough ships to sail home and retire as a rich man for the rest of his life.

Whatever the size of the Great Army was, we can be sure that it was a force to be reckoned with. It was large enough to defeat four kingdoms in England. Ivar the Boneless came not just to pillage but for conquest and he brought more than enough men to do just that.

Ivar's Victory Against King Ælla

"The point of revenge is not in the completion but in the process."

–Park Chan-wook

The Great Viking Army landed in East Anglia in the latter end of the year 865 AD. You can say that this was the starting point of their invasion. The locals were no match for the invading army. They were not prepared for any such onslaught.

One historian described the situation as the land being ripe for the pickings. The land was not united under one banner or one king. Instead it was divided amongst four warring factions or kingdoms. There was no standing army and the people and the kingdom was only defended by the fyrds.

Note that fyrds weren't hired and professional soldiers. They were local citizens that did the soldiering part time. In fact, these fyrds only expected to do the soldiering work for only 40 days. When Ivar and his men landed the sheer number of their force caused the East Anglians to panic.

In a bid to save their lives and to enact peace with the invading army, they promised to provide the Vikings with horses. They wintered there that year and prepared to march into Northumbria towards the end of 866.

Peace wasn't easily achieved and the Vikings raided. Along the way one village fell after the other. And in the year 867 the Vikings were now enabled with horses and could now leave the safety of their ships. They made their way deeper into the English interior.

Note that even though the Vikings were never really cavalry men, the horses that they obtained allowed them to move about with greater mobility. This meant that they were now better able to move from one target to the next. They were now better able to elude opposing forces.

This is also where we can see the tactician in Ivar the Boneless. He would at times order his men to fake a retreat. The defending soldiers of East Anglia will then pursue them and would usually over commit their pursuit. While the enemy forces were thinned out they would be ambushed by the Vikings. This was actually one of the many tactics that Ivar used to trap his enemies. He also devised other means to trap and confuse his enemies and also to avoid capture.

By the year 867 Ivar and his army of Vikings captured York. King Ælla was also unprepared for the incoming Viking invaders. He was already enmeshed in a war himself. He usurped the throne from King Osberht before and now they were deep in civil war.

The Ivar and his men conquered York, the two warring kings agreed to put aside the war for now and fight the common foe. Tradition puts it that Ivar did not win against King Ælla at first. So he put his diplomatic prowess to good use. He met with King Ælla for a truce. Ivar even made his men to stand down and to look like they were all just merry making and getting drunk.

That caused King Ælla to lower his guard and eventually meet Ivar. This was of course a trap and the result is that the king was captured and the rest of his forces defeated. King Osberht himself was killed in the ensuing conflict.

Now, there is a bit of confusion in the record. In some records it is said the English were all slaughtered in this incident, including both kings. However, we also have Norse sources that every single one of the English forces were killed but Ælla was captured.

The sagas also mention that Ivar sought to have some sort of reconciliation with King Ælla and only asked for land the size of an ox hide. This hide supposedly was sliced by Ivar so thinly that it was able to encompass an entire fortress. Again, the records become confusing at this point. However, we can be sure that King Ælla of Northumbria was definitely defeated by the Ivar and the Great Viking Army.

The Blood Eagle

"If an injury has to be done to a man it should be so severe that his vengeance need not be feared."

–Niccolo Machiavell

The way that King Ælla was tortured and executed is another matter of dispute among scholars and experts. The sagas say that Ivar the Boneless and his brothers performed the blood eagle on him. The way the blood eagle was performed is interestingly detailed in the Scandinavian sagas and other sources from the same area. The personal involvement of Ivar the Boneless is also heavily stressed in these records.

Here is an example of the graphic detail of such an execution from ßáttr af Ragnars sonum – it has been translated into English below:

"They caused the bloody eagle to be carved on the back of Ælla, and they cut away all of the ribs from the spine, and then they ripped out his lungs."

Among the Vikings this was a form of ritual murder. They called it the blood eagle because the corpse of the man that was subjected to it would look like a mangled eagle with its wings spread out. It was a slow and brutal death – not to mention extremely painful.

The practice of course is rejected by some academics. They say that the practice of the blood eagle is nothing more than plain folk lore. Some even say that the later descriptions were the result of mistranslations or perhaps problems with the transmission of the text. One expert observes that as the years move forward since the 9th century, the details about the blood eagle ritual from the sagas and the other similar Norse sources become more detailed and the process eventually got longer. A lot of the descriptions of the blood eagle ritual can be gleaned from 12th to 13th century sources – again already centuries removed from the time when it was carved on the back of King Ælla.

However, it cannot be denied that the term blood eagle is quite a meaningful concept in the Old Norse. The fact that it became a ritual method of slaying (more like filleting someone) indicates that the practice may be part of the local culture.

Note that the procedure described in the annals show a slow and graphic method of torture. Although we can't determine exactly when the practice was started, it cannot be denied that it had a long tradition in Ivar's Scandinavia. The records also indicate that this mode of torture and capital punishment was reserved for the most heinous of crimes.

How the Ritual Was Performed

The person who was to receive the blood eagle on his back was to be put down on his knees and his arms tied to posts. His arms would have to be spread apart in a wide embrace. The traditional interpretation was to have the blood eagle carved with the victim's lungs and ribs pulled out eventually. The idea is to make a bloody eagle out of the man being punished.

The ribs at the back of the man being punished will be detached from the back bone. The ribs would be spread wide making them look like wings on either side of the man being tortured. The lungs would then be pulled out and spread over the ribs thus giving the impression of bloody wings. Thus the body would look like a bloody mutilated eagle.

However, there are other accounts where the eagle was only carved on the back of the man without actually breaking any of his back bones. The eagle would have to look like it had its wings stretched out. Salt would then be rubbed against the wounds to intensify the pain. To finish things off, the man's chest would be cut open from the front and then the lungs would have to be pulled out. That would then make him look like a winged creature only that the wings were at the front.

A Sacrifice to Odin

The ritual of the blood eagle served more than just ritual killing or torture. The person being blood eagled was supposedly a sacrifice to the war god, Odin. Of course King Ælla wasn't the only person to receive the blood eagle. The Orkneyinga Saga also records other similar rituals performed and just as what happened to the king, these blood eagles were also done as an act of vengeance as well as an offering to the Odin.

Another detail that we should mention here is that in order to receive the blood eagle one must have done something completely honor-less. It should also be noted that in the sagas the ritual is called the blood eagle but in some it is also referred to as the blood owl as in Frithiof's Saga.

The Death of Ivar the Boneless

"Leaders should lead as far as they can and then vanish. Their ashes should not choke the fire they have lit."

–H. G. Wells

The death of Ivar the Boneless is said to have occurred in the year 871. Some records his death in 873. Æthelweard, Anglo-Saxon chronicler records his death in the year 870. But one thing is clear, by the year 870 the contemporary chronicles and the annals no longer mention Ivar as the leader of the Great Viking Army.

Some records state that Ivar went back to Viking controlled Dublin where he renewed his alliance with Olaf the White. There Ivar took upon him the title of King of the Northmen of All Ireland and Britain. It is ironic that a truly violent man would live the remainder of his life in peace.

The sagas mention that Ivar ordered that he should be buried in an area that was easily exposed to attack. He even prophesied that if their enemies should attack his grave they will have ill-success. It would appear according to the sagas that this prophecy by Ivar remained true until William I of England came. He successfully broke Ivar's burial ground, took the man's body, and burned it.

To the world Ivar the Boneless was one of the most cruel invaders and warriors the world will ever know. To the Vikings however, he was one of the greatest leaders that have brought glory to his people. His actions unwittingly helped to forge the unity of the lands he invaded and eventually helped to sow the seeds of that country.

Printed in Great Britain
by Amazon

80046869R00037